AGE OF FORGIVENESS

Sundress Publications • Knoxville, TN

ISBN: 978-1-951979-51-5
Library of Congress: 2023941399
Published by Sundress Publications
www.sundresspublications.com

Book Editor: Tennison Black
Managing Editor: Tennison Black
Editorial Assistant: Kanika Lawton
Editorial Interns: Max Stone, Lyra Thomas

Colophon: This book is set in Bembo Std.

Cover Design: Kristen Ton

Cover Art: Kristen Ton and Caleb Curtiss

Book Design: Erin Elizabeth Smith

AGE OF FORGIVENESS

Caleb Curtiss

Acknowledgements

Thanks to the editors at the following journals who first published the poems listed below, sometimes under different titles and in different forms. Some of the poems that appear in this book were included in a chapbook published by Black Lawrence Press.

Aquifer: The Florida Review Online: "III: (still be still)" and "IV: (I SPEAK WITH TONGUES)"
Beloit Poetry Journal: "Tilt"
Black Lawrence Press: "Elegy," "Still"
Diode: "Doe"
Gigantic Sequins: "Self-Portrait without My Dead Sister"
Green Mountains Review: "Self-Portrait in an Empty Swimming Pool"
Harpur Palate: "Gun"
Hobart: "I Am Whole, I Am Whole," "Possum"
Image: "Self-Portrait with a Stranger's Baby"
The Literary Review: "Peripeteia in Goltzius' Icarus"
New England Review: "Primer," "Poem"
Passages North: "Moth"
Pithead Chapel: "Excavation"
Quiddity: "Guncotton"
Redivider: "Time Capsule"
The Rupture: "Visitation," "Pincers"
Southern Humanities Review: "A Primal Sea"
Spork: "Self-Portrait with my Dead Sister," "Self-Portrait as a Photograph of My Father"
storySouth: "White Squall"
Tar River Poetry: "Sparrow"
The Southern Review: "Host of Hosts"
Thrush: "Cup & Saucer"
Valparaiso Poetry Review: "A Kind of Purple"
Weave: "Dream"
Witch Craft Magazine: "I: Rabbit" and "V: YOU ARE SAFE NOW"

"Time Capsule" was selected as winner of the Folger Adam's Prize.

Table of Contents

I

II

III

IV

V

ow we'll all be brothers of
The fossil fire of the sun.

ow we'll all be sisters of
The fossil blood of the moon.

–Jason Molina

e survivor imagines that she can transcend her rage
l erase the impact of the trauma through a willed,
iant act of love. But it is not possible to exorcise the
uma, through either hatred or love.

ıdith Herman

I

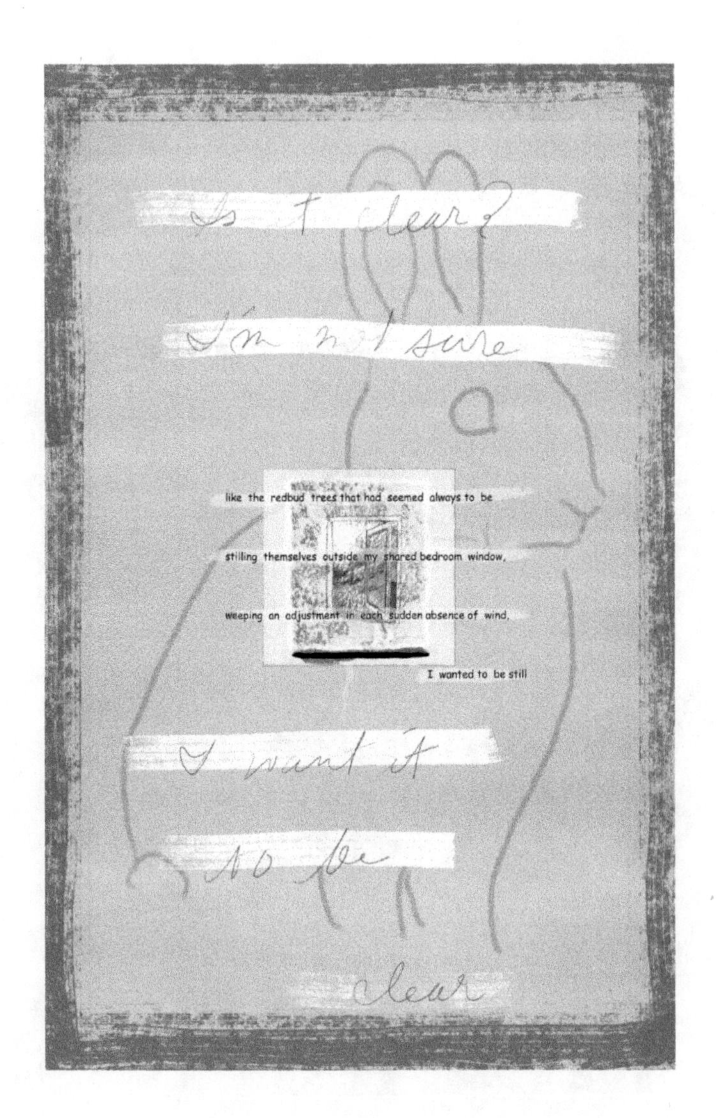

Is t clear?
I'm n t sure
like the redbud trees that had seemed always to be
stilling themselves outside my shared bedroom window,
weeping an adjustment in each sudden absence of wind,
I wanted to be still
I want it
to be
clear

ɔssum

: still, the possum says.
either twitch of tail

r flutter of eyelid.
on't move, she says,

d know how the world
your soggy milk carton,

ur cast off box of greasy takeaway,
len nest of robin eggs.

: still
d know how this moment
an oyster shell

ailing back at you
e the slit across your abdomen
m where

ur kits will crawl
climb onto your back
d into the world,

inking fondly of you, of the thirteen
pples arranged in a circle

the flesh of your belly,
the fifty

teeth God crammed inside
your marsupial head.

hoto Shot on Undeveloped Film

Vith white teeth
t behind a pink smile,

ou can see him there . . . sorry:
e *me* there, my face

ast in a golden light, a boy
a lime green tee-shirt

aptured in Kodacolor, eyes
arrow, squinting

eneath the low sun
f his tenth or eleventh summer.

Iis second-hand
Iuffy, red, rests

n its side on the green grass
f his front lawn;

is palms on its worn rubber grips,
e poses for his older sister, her face

bscured by a black box,
camera body. A glint in the lens,

he adjusts her position until
ve see him clearly.

A Kind of Purple

He veers from his path,
toward the canal's steep bank,

camera in hand, wearing brand new
trail shoes, a pair of khaki

cargo shorts, and a white crewneck
adorned with black lines that cross

over one another in a pattern
not unlike the wet marks

a child's finger will make
upon the thawing frost

of a car window, to chase down
a seagull, of all things.

What he wants from all this
is anyone's guess.

Probably just a picture: the bird,
a placeholder for something

he still can't name. See
the flowers that separate him

from the water? Hopeful yellow
somethings,

dious in the afternoon's dull light. Sprigs
preserved lace, funereal and fragile.

ney mope in the mud while the gull, feigning
ghtlessness, steps past.

nly after he drops his camera
the length of its strap, lets it

an his body forward slightly, like
nillstone cut for beginners,

ad takes toward the docks,
all the rest of us, birds and bench-sitters,

lax long enough to feel
ow the air has shifted in this poem:

owers that are not exactly
ght clusters of lilac blossoms—but still,

like those that grew from the slender
one structure of the tree

y father planted in his front yard
ter he lost his eldest daughter,

e lost
y big sister—

op their heads, bowing to the pressure
their own elaborate weight.

Excavation

I.

The past keeps coming back
and there's nothing we can really
do about it.

Foodstuffs and animals, mostly:

A fourteen-thousand-year-old loaf of bread,
intact in the paleosols of the Sahara.

A forty-thousand-year-old foal,
flawless in the Siberian permafrost.

And in the same crater as that horse,
they found the head of a baby lion,

smaller than a Chicago softball, still
covered in downy fur, his mouth

smooth with teeth yet to break gums.

*

Of course, you know that people, too,
are found like this, given new names

and put on display like
carnival oddities.

*

'oday, a three-thousand-year-old
'heel of cheese

ulled from the mouth of a Jordanian tomb,
nd I can hear my father laugh to himself
as he says it:

a little old, but still good.

II.

A boy lifts to his mouth
an ancient bite

of Hamburger Helper
he balances atop a spoon that,

to this day, can be found
in his parents' kitchen.

        He sits at the edge
of a dining room table

that's started to bow,
right there in the middle,

beneath the weight of their unopened mail:
two, maybe even three years of it, his surname

repeated
again and again behind the plastic

windows of unpaid bills, over
the sheen of junk mail selling two for one

pizza specials. An ad
for bicycles. Another

for weed killer. A paper
napkin rests in his lap while he dines,
Sisyphean, indifferent.

*

And yet,
s empty spoon disappears into his bowl,

en reappears
ıl.

ow can we not call this a miracle?

*

he cardboard box his noodles came in
s on the kitchen counter, archived

r the ages, its expiration date
vered by a thick line of black

k from the felt-tip
a food bank Sharpie.

*

e could be a statue now:
verboiled macaroni resting on a spoon,
ndered in unfinished limestone.

III.

Every day, a barefoot walk
        upon the gravel path

  would lead
to the property's edge,

the lapsed garden kept there,
        the site of summers-long

  excavations: the shallow
network of short tunnels,

each hole too narrow
for a growing body to squeeze through.

*

What had I been looking for?
No curling yellow paper

slid through the open mouths
and into the narrow caverns

of the bottles exhumed.

Some came up whole,
but most were broken,

their bodies
                cold from an Earth
that held them like children

ıd kept them there, under its weight,
until they broke.

Home School

How the redbud out front
would sieve the morning light in
through the living room window
and onto a map
of an imagined world indexed
in back of the NIV bible
spread open on my lap.

Here
is where the Nile overflowed
with blood, the sites of plague
and of famine, darkness,
disease—an age before the age
of forgiveness, before
there was a word for it—back

when swords and staffs, disguised
as fallen sticks, called out to me
from our unmown lawn,
an antistrophe whispered
in rabbit and squirrel,
in horsefly and garter snake.

Here
the slow drip of old pipes
forms a landmass
that spreads itself out on the ceiling
above me, a new continent
rendered in sepia, darkest at its center

d surrounded by an ocean
soft white plaster.

Gun

The gun my sister's husband used
to keep her in line

back before she went
and killed herself (by accident

or on purpose, I never really knew)
was small, nickel-plated, and cheap.

Why would it have to be anything else?
Although, I don't know if I should say *was.*

Guns are one of those things
that never really fall out of style.

One owner passes theirs on to the next,
no one but a criminal throws their gun away.

Anyhow, he pointed it at me once, just for fun.
We were on his couch

getting to know one another.
He talked and then I talked.

We were having a nice time.
He talked, and then,

while I talked, a dark
aperture, narrow as a No. 2

encil eraser appeared before me,
nd I laughed.

was like I had expected him to do
ust what he had done: apropos of nothing,

reach into the crevasse between
is oversized sofa cushions,

ull out a little handgun
nd point it at me.

Vas it loaded or not loaded? I didn't know!
nd so, I laughed: ha-ha. It was a joke!

Ie laughed, too: ha-ha.
laughed and he laughed, and then,

ve both stopped laughing,
nd then, still smiling—click.

Sparrow

My sister
is not a woman, a girl, or even

a real someone or something.
Not anymore.

In her place
I find a bird, nearly

frozen, lying in a field,
its body

broken in some way,
utterly flightless

and possibly a sparrow—
any bird would be

a curious replacement—
but this bird

is like her,
and also like a child. Its body

trembles like a child's
as if it has lost something

irretrievably warm,
something simple.

is dying, of course,
.t also

; the kind of thing
at she, as a child,

ould be moved
care for. The kind of thing

could never look at.
Even now,
I know

could use this moment, this
ing thing to remember her,

at I don't want to.

II

isitation

'en the wire-thin filament in our night-light
ıs a kind of memorial back then,

artifact of the nights
: saw him there, his form

ıfting in the shadows cast upon our bedroom walls,
ıngs rising as if to fly—but did he ever fly?

, *maybe* a bird, but maybe not a bird
cause, just as easily, he might have been

ınake; a serpent, emergent
əm the narrow mouth

' a tall urn, or a vessel crafted to resemble
e body of a swan. Wings, not wings,

ıt the semblance of wings
ifting on the wallpaper as we slept,

y sister and I, dreaming the dreams
e living dream.

What was he then
ıt a god of origins unknowable?

is row after row of feathers, dark
ıd barbed like plates of armor: scapulars

and coverts, alulas and tertials,
the long quills at the ends,
dark organs of his flight.

Tilt

We walked the rows of our strip mall arcade to find it waiting for us: Mortal
ombat: verboten machine in its inaugural summer. Nineteen-Ninety-two:

The year it swallowed its very first coins. I hesitated, but not much,
As he pinned me there in front of the screen, this man, just barely a man,

Recent discharge from the local children's home & new subject of my
arents' amateur ministry. He stood, shifting slowly behind me

With his block-kick-jump-duck. His hands over mine as he ripped the spine
rom our opponent's back. He never let them fall intact, never left them

Where they knelt before him. He who moved into our basement with his
Plastic sack of dirty clothes, his no toothbrush, no soap, his Nintendo

Entertainment System & said he'd stay long enough to get up & on
His feet. My parents washed his feet & prayed for him as he sat on our couch

Draped in my father's bathrobe. They left us alone with him, let us play
games
With him—my sister his favorite challenger, but I might serve too.

Eyes glued to pixeled pools of blood, the other consoles blathered on behind
us
& I knew I wasn't to play this one. *But look*, he said, *we can do it*

If you want. If you just don't tell. & *How well can you keep a secret?*
Well, I said. *Sure*, I said, his fingers soft if heavy upon my own—

The buttons' plastic slap whenever he attacked—he showed me how
It was a game of rhythm: knowing when it's safe to strike & when you are

Exposed, you always give yourself an out, a way to dodge the blows.
& even if I liked it, standing with my back to him as he taught me

To slay all who stood in our path, later that same day, I did not keep
My no-tell promise. & yes, I liked that too. The telling. Revealing him

As the liar he was as we sat at the dinner table: his face grown
Red, his empty plate, my parents' trembling jaws. My silent sister, knifing

Her peas, crushing their skulls.

iants, When They Corner You,
ill Rip You Limb from Limb

aid my hand upon that page held it

In place for as long as I could a book

it and illustrated for kids like me

wound had yet to open fatal if

Invisible upon Goliath's head

boy's thrown stone exposed field a bright sky

inted in behind them like a drop-screen

In an awkward family photo Saul out

f frame fretting in his tent as this man

ifted me on his lap his hand around

My wrist: *say*   *what you think it sounded like*

lap of stone on skull brief hush in the wake

f his fall low hum of sudden knowing

See how there's a moral to this story?

Black Swan

I saw one once, even
if I can't tell you much about him.
Not because he made me

swear some graven oath (swans
can't do that kind of thing) but because
I don't remember, really.

The way it feels now, it's as if,
before we ever met, he'd already
spun himself into being

deep inside the coiled tissue
of a dream, back when dreams
seeped past the boundary of the mind,

when moments still
took shape as dreams. More like,
he did harm as a god will do harm

when he adopts his earthly form
as a man, but even
as a lamb, a swan with wings,

dark like those of an angel
sent to ravage one
but not another household

entirely, to spare some
but not other bodies,
as a means to ravage

our household entirely.
Even if I don't remember,
I know how he showed himself

› my sister
ıd gave himself to me
ı a form I couldn't see.

A Primal Sea

The firmament would tremble from time to time.
His basement bedsheets, a kind of memory.

> How he held your body down, a memory
> I don't have. Something I have to imagine:

Rain for days, our street submerged—imagine
Noah fucked up and put his phone on silent—

> What then? Immersed in his absence, his silent
> Schemes, our house imbued with muffled screams.

A darkening voyage christened with screams
That echoed off his mast. But, in real life,

> God hadn't any time for phone calls, his life
> Full with the promises he kept in those days.

Tell me, sister, how you kept in those days.
The firmament trembles from time to time.

od Forgives

'en those among us who are least deserving?

Yes.

10se who would take up arms against their neighbors?

Yes.

10se who would make from their bodies weapons of indescribable
tential, unimaginable destruction?

Yes.

10se who would board in the basement of a family's home?

Yes.

are with them their meals, their small moments of joy?

Yes.

1d at night, rise like a specter.

Yes.

hose who would ransack a child's body?

Yes.

girl's small body?

Yes.

'hat happens to that girl? To the space she leaves behind?

Cup & Saucer

Four years old, sun sick
and unaware of what the ocean will take,
my brother clambered up
the Cup and Saucer:
two rocks stacked one on top of the other:
one the size of a Buick, the other below it
a full-sized van
overlooking Buzzard's Bay.

Not knowledge, but knowing: the kind
of knowing that overcame me upon seeing him there,
looking down as the tide sucked at the rocks,
the barnacles, a full story beneath his toes:
the calmness that comes in knowing how the world
could change suddenly, irrevocably.

Fifteen years later,
after picking him up from his shift,
I remind him of this
before telling him how our sister, Elisabeth,
who had been sunbathing further down the pier,
hadn't made it to the other side
of an intersection that morning.

Of course, when I'm finished,
there isn't anything worth saying
and we're left with what we're always left with:
the line that separates then and now,
the line that threads together our moments,
pricking through us as it goes.

ɅIoth

etween your tongue and soft palate,
ou hold it like an oblong bead,

icturing
our sister, your freshman year of high school,

er sixteenth birthday—a day you spent
oled up in your bedroom

fter getting caught
ith grain alcohol
n your Gatorade bottle.

'ou hold it

like it's her marriage,
cardboard box of old diaries,

photo of her as the driver
f a black Oldsmobile Cutlass

Ciera, circa

few years before side-impact
irbags were really a thing.

'ou hold it,
etting it go numb in your mouth,
retending it's not

a shot of Old Crow, Rebel Yell,
whatever it actually is, pretending

it's grain alcohol and wanting it
to burn a little more,

and so
you flatten it across your tongue, let it

burn a little more
until your mouth goes numb again, before

your throat shudders like a memory,

something
that doesn't belong to you: a young woman's wardrobe:

dresses and sweaters,
blouses—all that stuff,

swaying on their hangers like ghosts.

Had she been in a rush when she first saw it?

A misappropriation of light
in the upper-left pocket of her favorite

tee-shirt
reveals itself after a morning shower.

The work of a moth?

A tear in the folding room?

Let's say
e wears it anyway,

ves her confusion some time
to falter, grow

into anger.

'atch
hile she churns through each
rment in her closet.

ote
ow the absent fabric
cumulates—note

weight—
how she resists.

ou hold it
like a threat,

the unvoiced
lict you witnessed when you last saw her:

1ake 'n Bake dinner,
ree cups of instant coffee.

er husband, clicking
nickel-plated sub-
ompact in every direction

like a kid
with a cap gun,

pointing it at you,
at your sister,
her cat, her couch.

Afterwards,
        he'll assure you it wasn't loaded.

No bullets! No bullets! No bullets,
I swear! Plus he'd removed the firing pin

                                        earlier that day.

You want to feel it
in your mouth again,

hold it
        like a firing pin,

like each
twenty-two caliber vacancy left in that closet,

let its shape feel as sharp, as succinct,
  as a husband's jealous rage:

you imagine him
indignant, letting her believe that each hole

                                had been the work of a moth,

so you hold it

like a voiceless glottal fricative, each

prayer strung together at her funeral.
An utterance

etached from its referent,

presence that will burn

long after it's passed.

Self-Portrait with a Stranger's Baby

Li'l body, all packed up, bright with white lights,
A green strand of broken glass, sidewalk-strewn.
Who would just leave a baby Jesus out
On their front lawn for anyone to take?
Lungs spent up, crackling like the cinders
That *snap-pop* beneath my strip-soled sneakers.
I run until I forget where I am—
Leave the lights behind and hold his body
Close to mine: small, dark, hollow, hard. I was
Lost and Mary knew it. Her stare impugnes
Crudely from the crudeness of that crude die
In which her form was cast—bewildering
Sight—her image shrinking in the glow
That lights the rising expanse between us.

III

REMEMBER
I DID SEE
ONE ONCE
I CAN'T TELL
YOU MUCH
ABOUT HIM
listen
he
will
not
spare
our household

rimer

here was an actual noise,
mething I will never hear,
d then, I am told, she died.

his is the only important part:
hat prepares us,

a primer—

ot physical, though not precisely
religious experience either.

knowing, reinforced by the absence
f a body: an erasure, and then,
vacuum: space

verberating like steel
n steel, a place
here there could have been

ore
an a body fallen,

a body fallen from.

Time Capsule

I stopped listening, not wanting a new emergency,
but also, not wanting another

old emergency to return, not wanting these things
to pull me into the air like a body

moored to the ocean's surface, a buoy,
not wanting to be exposed. So,

like a body of water beneath a storm,
I developed a healthy fear

of electricity—how it could flow
through some perfect, theoretical conduit

like a breeze, invisible and pushing itself
through a vacuum. Like

the redbud trees that seemed always to be
stilling themselves

outside my shared bedroom window,
weeping an adjustment into each

absence of wind, I wanted to be still:
to surround myself

in a bronzed web of baby's breath, to cover myself
in the stasis of weakened verbs, to be

transferable. Or maybe, I just wanted to be
transferred, made into a sack

of bone meal, a pail of sand: to have purpose,
or to give myself some future purpose,

agary I could crawl inside of
these years later, a gift to my adult self,

absence in the center of a memory
iere order could exist without space,

ters could not die
d the past is always a red thing

ating away from me like a raft.
ke the sea in a storm, I did not know
w I was like a storm.

Self-Portrait With My Dead Sister

A girl and a boy are sitting on a curb
next to the ocean on a trip to Oregon

where the rain, which has just stopped,
has formed into a mud puddle right there

in the foreground, in front of the boy's white
shoe. His pants are blue, his jacket

is red, and he is not smiling at all, which
I think is what makes her faintly upturned
lip look so much like a smile. Never mind

that these people were real, that one
will grow up and keep on being real

while the other will grow up and be dead.

Never mind the very brusque presentation
the speaker employs. We might
excuse him on account of his grief.

Ignore him for now and stay with the facts.

Fact: the boy is nearly five, which makes
the girl seven, which makes it
15 years before she drove past a stop sign

and then didn't do anything ever again.

ut here it's different. Here,
here she has just turned up

ne corner of her lip, pulled
er legs to her chest,

ne rests her chin on her knees,
ıspicious of her own inertia,

ne static nature of her disposition.
Here, let it be enough to believe

nat she could look up at me, smile
real smile, and say something

enuinely irrelevant, something
won't pretend to understand.

Dream

This time you're not my sister,
but you're not a stranger either.

You're someone I don't know:
a little girl with a pixilated face

like a witness obscured
on a television news broadcast.

This time we sit on a train
while you describe

what bus transfers
and energy transfers have in common,

how people don't just cease to exist
when they get off a bus,

how they continue in their own
little worlds, like earthworms.

*

This time you talk to me like I'm a child,
put your fingers in my hair and explain
how we can only go in one direction at a time.

*

ıis time I'm sitting alone on a bus,
nembering advice you never gave me,
•w your teeth looked when you smiled.

*

ıis time I'm standing in the bathroom,
•lding your teeth in the palm of my hand.

*

ıis time you're in a car, driving through the country,
ı your way to drop off your husband's

ɔod pressure medication. I sit shotgun and listen
you say all the things that you say: that you're fine,

ittle tired, but fine. The radio is on
.d you're singing along, reaching for a cigarette
the console between us.

*

his time your lighter won't work,
ɔ matter how many times you spin its little wheel.

*

his time
you're asleep
ıd there's nothing I can do to wake you up.

*

This time the radio is static
but you nod your head,
sing along just the same.

*

This time you blow by the stop sign and everything's fine.

*

This time you blow by the stop sign and everything's fine.

*

This time you say how tired you are.

*

This time I'm at the bathroom mirror,
holding your teeth in my hand, feeling

how they grind together when I make a fist,
how your molars rub into each other

like lumps of chalk; your canines,
your incisors start to break skin.

*

This time I'm looking at my gums
in the mirror, trying to press *your*

eth into *my* mouth,
membering how you'd make me

it sand, did it often enough
hat I started to like it, started
eat it by myself—

ow my first set of teeth
smoothed over like river stones.

*

This time I hear *your* voice when I speak,
nd when my teeth fall out,
don't know where they came from.

*

Nowadays our referents don't match up.

Blue for me is red for you. Me?

I'm fine.
Content.
a touch

wiser having just
put the dog to sleep,

which I think
might be funny to you.
s it funny to you?

Next time
we won't speak at all,
just gaze into the void

the other has become.

*

Next time, I'll remind you to look both ways
before you cross the street,

like you did for me: the both of us

holding hands, fingers
laced through fingers—how long

did we wait to know it was safe?

ɜlf-Portrait Without My Dead Sister

ɔon serious reflection,
'e concluded that the day my sister died, all in all,
ılly wasn't such a bad day, per se: the weather
the allergy index & at least she was around
r part of it, & so on. Even beyond that,
was a moment of great hope & excitement for all,
also, who was I to mourn amid the hustle
the bustle & the various smeared beauty products
all those *no reallys* hanging on my mouth with
:es and ums, & etcetera. And also,
no was I to question the order of this new universe,
hich, despite my suspicion that it might just do so,
s kept on expanding in all of its bovine splendor,
ıving behind its quivers of matter, its great clumps
'long time.

Guncotton

Think of it
as something grayish (sparsely
defined (quivering
like a misaligned film reel
(Nitrocellulose (increasingly
diminutive (wrapped around itself
(a curling
(a corn snake's
sudden retreat
into itself (a hawk's
inward descent

Think of it broadly (as something
it is not (not
nothing (not absence (the vacuum
that sits like a specter
in your sister's space (corn field
(intersection (stop sign
(the irrevocable
trajectory of her Oldsmobile
(stop sign (black
skid marks over rural
asphalt

Think of it
as what these things
have become in your mind (vague
objects (plots on a graph (their relationship
predetermined (inevitable
so that now

ıeir collision can be beautiful
(something you can hold in place
(a frame
ut of context (something fragile
(soaked
in oil (kept safe
afe

as guncotton

IV

I SPEAK WITH TONGUES
They saw the young child and fell'd
him.
MORE THAN YOU ALL

Am Whole, I Am Whole

started watering the houseplants on a regular basis. This after watching ne dead multiply for the years I spent watering them on an *ir*regular basis. ou might be thinking just now that the sense of accomplishment I erived from all this must not have been overwhelming, and you'd be ght. Watering the houseplants was something I got to feel good about; 's the sort of thing that people ought to do: maintain a life that is not their wn life, provide one's self with a routine that supports the life one wants) lead: a set of reliable patterns that serve as an accurate representation of ne person you are and not just the person you imagine yourself to be.

asically, all that stuff the therapist says, but of course, I got pretty bored ith all that after a while. Sort of just decided, *what's the point?* And soon, started to do what people do when they become bored of watering their lants: over the course of several months, I created a new version of myself sing a complex procedure I found on the internet involving a bathtub nd no small amount of exfoliated skin and hair and shaved whiskers and lipped toenails, and so on, as well as several bottles of nearly expired ombucha (ginger!).

nd then suddenly, another me: *someone to water the plants!* Someone ho knows which plants require greater or lesser amounts of water; which lants benefit from a more syncopated watering schedule as opposed to an specially predictable one; which plants have succulent leaves in need of pritzing and which have waxy leaves in need of having mayonnaise ubbed into them monthly. (That, if you did not know, is something that eople do with their plants.) Someone who will not go on superfluous rives at night for hours at a time or smoke cigarettes in the backyard or e down on the couch and listen to the sound of his heartbeat inside his kull.

Someone who will engage in the good work of supporting my yucca, a plant I did not even know I had. *Hey, where did you come from, little Yucca?* No answer. OK. Anyway, I'd tend to the plants while reading a book in my bedroom or being tender with my wife or sitting outside on the porch and smoking a top-secret cigarette (or two), always returning to our common space in the living room. Always to find him leaving. *All for the better*, I'd think. *Really, there probably is only enough room for the one of us.*

On the rare occasion that we were in the same room together for more than a few seconds, we'd respectfully avert eye contact, thinking it only proper to give the other his space, allow him the illusion of aloneness. The poor fellow was, after all, just a recycled version of another version of himself. Time went on like this. The plants thrived, and so did I, in a way: each time I caught a glimpse of myself, I'd note that my body had somehow grown *into* itself—that's the only way I can put it: my arms looked like my arms, legs, legs, torso, torso, and so on, but there was also something different about them: a sense that they held their own weight in a way they hadn't quite done before. I felt like how Pinocchio probably felt pre-lying about a bunch of stuff, post-becoming a real boy.

One day, it must have been winter, because my trips to the porch had become less regular and it was very cold out, we found ourselves eating breakfast together, which was strange as I'd never seen him eat before. This made a kind of sense, because he and I were on different schedules: his, a plant watering schedule, mine a real-life schedule. But it also did not make sense because, don't you think I would've seen him at least once, before then, eat something? Anyway, I must not have found it to be too weird because that soon became our routine: breakfast every morning with myself!

An orange usually, and a cup of coffee. Some mornings we'd end up with a bigger than usual orange, in which case we'd split it. Toast some ɔrnings, not toast on other mornings. Casual stuff. Not a lot of talking, ally. No talking at all, really. More of a free exchange of thoughts. fortless. Probably just what you're imagining. Still, we were most mfortable inside each other's silences, the quiet that we let extend from e to the other: like a conversation, but not.

ıen, one day I decided to get healthy again. I said, *I'm gonna try to get althy again!* Kicked cigarettes, cut booze, paid special attention to my gestive tract. And for me, kombucha figures prominently into this part the process due to its high retail price and its probiotic mysteries. This erested me, and after reading the label, he had for me a question. *What a mother?* A good question. What *is* a mother? And sure, I had some swers, but they were the kind that make for even more questions, and is line of conversation, I could see, was sure to get sensitive, and so I read him from the label about how the drink was fermented, how the yeast d the bacteria at the top, which looks like a weird jellyfish, is called, of things, a mother. So, it was around this time that he stopped eating.

hat's the point? Daily, he could be found not watering or spritzing or ayonnaising the plants. Nightly, he'd sleep a light and disturbed sleep, cinated by how—no matter the number of times he'd previously atered and taken care of them—without his attention, the plants were rning: their leaves cupping into themselves, their edges crisping up like tle pepperonis. I made food for him to eat. Some of his favorites. *Caleb,* vould say, *eat for me this smoked pork pozole topped with a beautifully ɔached egg, this seared grouper cheek in a reduced yellow curry sauce rved upon a bed of perfectly prepared saffron rice. Caleb, eat for me this pperoni pizza that I ordered from your favorite pizza place. Caleb, please ɔp. Do not waste away anymore like our plants have begun to waste vay: even our mysterious yucca looks as if it will surely die. Caleb, do ɔt die.*

Force feeding did not work. You have probably tried to force feed someone something before, no? You know, then, how it is not the sort of thing that really works out too well in a scenario like this. Moreover, you know the ways in which you are powerless, even against your own will, much less the will of another. And so that is what I came to expect, or rather, allow: the slow degradation of the body, my body, a body I'd eventually come to hold in my hands and carry with me to bed at night, a body I would bathe with, walk with, hold with me for days and days, days on end, so many days until the day I thought he had died, and then even longer until the day I heard him whispering.

Dead, or alive, he was pleading with me, and no, not for food. Not for water, but pleading nonetheless. Caleb. Eat me, Caleb. Can you hear me? Is that you, Caleb? Eat me, Caleb. Eat me. Eat me. Eat me, Caleb. Even that mysterious Yucca we cared for together is dead, you can eat me now, and so on, and so on.

And so, I did.

V

ɔem

ıis poem has no occasion,
dited that part out.

ke a body, or a memory,
has rebuilt itself over time.

r, like the Argos, each of its component parts
ve, by this point, been exchanged for newer,

ore efficient ones. For example, now,
hen I overhear someone say the word

offee,"
u, sister, drink from your cup of coffee.

put the output, ad infinitum, I have become so
oficient, I have learned to master

e beuracracy of my grief, proceed
rmulaically. Resolved

at the function of your absence has grown
ss integral to my algorithm.

'hereas you aren't even *you* anymore.

Pincers

It is easy to regard the body as a text and not a reflection of the algorithm that brought it into being, a phantom limb affixed to the mind by lines like sutures, unseen. When she wanted to reach something beyond her armchair, I remember, my grandmother would extend a long metal arm, thin, a handle with a plastic trigger, with pincers at the end. The odd issue of *Time* left just out of her natural reach, yellow pill bottles, piled up on the desk near her chair. Sometimes she would use it to knock the phone off its cradle while I sketched in my sketchpad, and Phil Donahue continued his monologue, and she laid her head back and napped where she sat. Other times, she would use it to reach up and nudge the framed black and white photograph of my grandfather, kept just out of reach on the side table next to her chair—see him there, still standing back then, in his Army greens, a thin smile, the Belgian sky gone gray above him. His hands dangling at his sides, or were they tucked into his pockets, I can't remember which. The two-and-a-half-ton Studebaker idles behind him, at the same time a dim shadow passes over his face. See how a cloud of dust settles at his feet? And that shadow on his face? A plume of smoke, the slight structure of a wing circling above him, dividing a tranche of aging sunlight as the afternoon signals its retreat, through the windows of her apartment, the sky gone pink, threatening red.

elf-Portrait as a Photograph of My Father

oday, the seedpods on the milkweed that grows
ong the road between the airport and the place

here my grandparents will die, began to open themselves
nperceptibly, as if each were the beak of a baby crane

: the first change in pressure that comes
ith their mother's circling descent.

saw them like this from the window
f my father's Buick, watched

hile each of them passed us by, their cracked
iouths and eyeless heads, and I decided to do

hat I do best, and I kept my mouth shut.
oon, after watching my father stand in unsteady synchrony

ith his father, I will lift myself from the couch
ı the lobby and head for the patio where I will stand

t my father's left hand, his father's right, and I will smile
ɔr the camera, not noticing how the seeds on the silver

ıaple behind us have matured. How some
ave already detached themselves from the branches

o begin their slow spiral downward. Because we feel
pressure in the air, something that tells us

we are mortal, that we will be here forever, we smile
these facsimile smiles, lips taut over straight white teeth.

eripeteia in Goltzius' *Icarus*

is evidenced here in the fact of his falling,
re in the arrogant tilt of his nose and here

the slight fold of scrotum, of testicle
t visible—clutched between his curiously

irless legs as his curiously hairless body
overcome by its eternal weight, its eternal

l, which occurred to me the first time I saw it,
I saw in him a timeless guilt, an eternal

ilt, and for me there was a sudden guilt
nply in having seen him this way—a thing

verted, not just a reflection—a duplication
a duplication.

White Squall

Fact: the stove grew
cool that night, as the logs
burned to embers—

the sky had fallen much
lower & closer to their home
than it ever had before.

The dark cornfield
rattled in its frame as,
switch in hand,

her mother urged her
through the open door
of their rented

farmhouse, slammed it
shut & turned
the deadbolt as the storm

approached. The girl
leaned into a frozen wall
of rotten clapboards.

This—more than the weeks
that would pass
with her mother locked

ɜainst her will in a state
ıental institution—this
what I understood to be

ıe source of *my* mother's rage,
ıe screaming white
ɜnter of it, my inheritance

om that little girl, dressed
ı threadbare pajamas,
ɔandoned

ı her own mother's
lence as the blizzard
rew closer.

And then,
hile waiting for the additional
reamers she has asked

ıe busboy to bring
ɔr her still-too-dark
offee, my mother corrects

ıe record, tells me, *yes,*
his happened, but not to me.
ınd how could this be?

Ay memory of her memory
ıas played a trick on me,
ıy timing off

by an entire generation:
it had been *her* mother, Helen,
left in the cold that night.

Her broken hairpin
that petitioned the lock
as it froze into place,

the field like a sea of froth
come to swallow her whole.

egy

ound you
a beach this time,
ng with your heels

its shoreline,
ur back
sh with the changing sand,

d you were staring at me,
t not with your normal eyes,
th these cowry shells:

e your eyes,
t not.

was cold, and you lay there,
ody
the beach, my sister

d not my sister,
e shells, your eyes,
ll as stone thumbs,

gile even, as if
e slightest movement,
bump in the road,

ould have them
ll from your face.

I wait for you to stir, to breathe
but you couldn't have known

I was sitting there, waiting,
couldn't have felt the ribbed

arc of those shells
pressed into the flesh
of your eyelids.

And then,
not suddenly,
          you were sitting.

Or,
you'd been sitting all along,
and because

the sun was setting,
making the horizon
more of an idea

than something
either of us could point to,
we sat together,

the shore
washing over our feet:
first our heels

and then our toes. So
cold, but we watched it rise
and did not move

it filled the space
:tween us, defining our divisions
a strait divides land.

*

ou lay on a beach, a bundle
f synapses.

/aves sway over you,
ack and forth,

ke the chassis
f an overturned car,

1 Oldsmobile
eadying herself

eside a corn field,
stop sign.

memory
ooped like tape
1 a cassette,

orn out
ith play,
our sand pale

ill of mollusks,
ieir shells

shimmering
like toenails
in the afternoon sun;

you threw
a handful of them

into the air
like confetti,
like coins in a well,

a memory half-lost
in the twisting synapses

of a moment past:
the present tense

of your absence
tangible for a moment
and then not, lost

but not done, waiting
like I waited for you

behind a stack of rocks
so I could go *boo!*
startle you

so you'd stumble in the sand,
hate me for a moment,
my laughter

ıshing away
the sound of the waves
around us just now,

ing once more, reciting
in perpetuity
a necessary erosion.

Still

Still

the house

Still

the room

Still

the couch

the sheets

the chest

bending up

and down

as a field

in a mirror

And still

the mind

if in

a moment

waiting

r

casting

hat

can't be

rgotten

Still

ie phone

the spinning

heel

of a car

1 a ditch

Still

ie body

unseen

huddering

still

1 the mind

still

1 the mind

the mind

is still

even now

be still.

elf-Portrait in an Empty Swimming Pool

our sister curls her fingers
.o your hair, makes her hands
:o fists and holds them there.

has just stopped
ning, and neither of you
n look at the other, plus

u are dumbstruck. These
e swim trunks? And so this
ust be a pool.

he pool in which your big
ter once held your head under water—half-
artedly tried to drown you.

hlorine in the eyes, sodium
rbonate, you keep them closed
e you are praying,

e the water surrounding you
divine, a new kind of air
at you will learn

breathe inside of,
e temperature of these new
mensions familiar somehow

you make yourself stop
eling altogether
w her fingers are still

in your hair, how,
this time, you feel them pulling you up
and there is nothing you can do

to stop this from happening:
the warmth that surrounds you
at the moment you break the surface,

that old air reminding you
of how cold you have been,
of how the dead always, eventually,

become tropes of the living, and so
are made all the more dead
by virtue of having lived,
and by virtue of their being dead.

Iost of Hosts

Iy son reaches into the refrigerator for a peach.
3all," he says.

Peach," I say.
is easy to be precious

ntil you aren't much of anything anymore.
Iot long ago in Kunming, China,

ıey found the fossilized remains of a peach
om 2.6 million years ago.

was, at some point, all
ut identical to the one my son is holding.

'he moment they unearthed it,
vept from it a layer of ancient dust,

ıe sky would've allowed
ɔr the sun's crepuscular rays

ɔ shine down upon it as if to suggest an arrival.
'hese days, the sea, when I see it

ı pictures obtained by way of my more uninspired
ıternet browsing, looks

articularly bored. "Same as any other day,"
: seems to say. "Ball," my son says,

nd he takes a bite. How is it
hat you have come so far?

Iow is it that you have form?
ınd what is flesh if not a carrier?

A bearer of genetic material?
A host or a messenger sent

from the unrecognizable, holding at its core
something we might recognize: duplication,

a way of penetrating
the moment in all of its dreary infinity.

I don't worry that his teeth
will graze over, or even

bear down upon that tight
walnut of a pit

as they pass through its skin: soft, sweet.
There are ways of knowing: learning,

having learned;
those are some of the ways.

Today, in the afternoon of this,
our second January, I wake up

and somehow the moon
is the same as it's ever been,

casting its calcified rays
down upon me as if to suggest an arrival.

Even here, in a loneliness
that is not quite aloneness,

each thing I have let myself be
is present, with me: "Peach," I say.

oe

ıose who saw remember hearing him first: a light clap of hooves on the eet-pavers like rounds from a cap gun or the sound a stone will make ıen dropped on a much larger stone. The night before there was a heavy n that sat in the fields until dawn when it rose a heavy fog. He must have en confused, turned around by the fog, or perhaps he came to us by way the fog, the long heavy rain from the night before hanging over us like a ecter, a visitor.

ıose who saw told of an enormous crown of horns, others of dark eyes like yx spheres set deep in his narrow head like marbles pressed into the dirt a boot. The fog kept our doors closed and so it was a small group of men ho gathered, holding long guns, adorned in heavy garments used to stalk the fields, near the lake, in the woods that spread into the distance, past e edge of town. The echoes of men hushed through the streets, ears tuned r the clap of hooves on pavement. We looked from our windows, hushed the shuffle of their long slow steps up the street, past the bank, past the hool, past the fueling station, all closed for the fog which grew so thick the en couldn't see what lay in their path and so began to move as one.

went on like this for some time, fruitless and boring, but soon became uch easier work than any of them could have imagined: the buck not a ıck at all but the small, heaving body of a doe, her scent already deep inside e dogs: loam and wet leather, clotting blood, a hint of wood smoke. The ɔgs had to be heeled, their looped chains grinding deep into the thick fur their necks. Perplexed, the men stepped forth to look at her—a body at st at the edge of a field, small and new to winter, trembling with eyes osed like those of a child at the edge of sleep—and softened at the sight of er, fur-covered flesh coiled over adolescent bone. One man began to shion a bridle made from the length of rope he brought for the buck. nother leaned down to slide the knotted line into her mouth. She quaked hile the men nodded, watching her rise as a marionette will rise once its ırtain is drawn up.

s she stood, so stood the fog. So stood the dogs, seeing in her what the en had missed—missed or ignored, the doe's eyes set deep and dark in her

head. Then, the bridle was on the ground and the doe was in the fiel
running as she had first been expected to run. The men were pleased to s
her in this way: a figure in motion behind a layer of thickening fog that ro
in the field, kept rising like steam from a kettle; the mud from the fiel
black, and heavy, slowed her gait like the thick mud of a dream, her path
once foreseeable to the men who watched her for a moment, cold in h
uneven grace, the tumbling sight of her bony frame unfolding in front
them.

She lay there all night, long after the men turned back, her absence risin
from the earth like smoke as the men, each with their families, washed an
ate and turned, all night, turning back, as echoes from the day find purcha
in our dreams.

Notes

ny of the poems, and all of the visual poems that appear in this book, after Nance Van Winckel.

Rabbit)": A visual poem made using digital illustration methods and a erpt of printed and scanned text from "Time Capsule."

Kind of Purple": The flowers mentioned in this poem are the flowers t grow on the banks of the canal in Dublin where it crosses under the band Bridge.

(he tamed Us)": A visual poem I made using digital illustration methods l a piece of religious ephemera left on my door in Champaign, Illinois in 17.

Primal Sea": This poem is a Duplex, which is a poetic form that nbines properties of the Ghazal and the Sonnet. Jericho Brown invented Duplex and made it popular with his book *The Tradition* (Copper nyon 2019).

I (still be still)": A visual poem I made using digital illustration methods l mixed media, including excerpts from my poems "Still" and "Black an."

/ (I SPEAK WITH TONGUES)": A visual poem I made using digital stration methods and mixed media, including ephemera from the gram of a children's nativity from the early 2010s. The handwritten se is from 1 Corinthians 14:18.

(YOU ARE SAFE NOW)": A visual poem I made using digital stration methods and mixed media, including a family photo and a otographed print that depicts a scene from Matthew 14:31: "Jesus mediately reached out his hand and caught him, saying to him, 'You of le faith, why did you doubt?'"

Thank You

is book owes a debt to all of my teachers, particularly Maryann Peshkin d Betty Rowell, the public educators who taught me to read and write.

vould like to thank the Delaware Division of the Arts and their staff for eir support. Special thanks to Aaron Burch, Nance Van Winckel, Tomás orín, and David Wojahn for their guidance on this project. Thank you Janice N. Harrington, Maggie Smith, Chen Chen, Jensen Beach, Jodee nley, Dave Housley, Becky Barnard, Julianna Baggott, Mark Cox, itlin Rae Taylor, Adam Voith, Connie May Fowler, Amish Trivedi, obert Hirschfeld, and Charlie Weinberg. And more than thanks to my fe, Sarah Curtiss.

e list of people who encourage me and help me grow as a person, a cher, and a writer is long—if you're reading this, you're probably on it. ank you so much.

nally, to Tennison S. Black, Erin Elizabeth Smith, Kristen Ton, Kanika wton, Lyra Thomas, Max Stone, and everyone at Sundress Publications, ank you for your labor, for believing in my poems, and for making my anuscript into a book.

About the Author

.eb Curtiss was born and raised in Champaign-Urbana, Illinois. He is the
hor of one previous chapbook, *A Taxonomy of the Space Between Us.*
lives with his family in Delaware.

Other Sundress Titles

Another Word for Hunger
Heather Bartlett
$16

Little Houses
Athena Nassar
$16

In Stories We Thunder
V. Ruiz
$16

Slack Tongue City
Mackenzie Berry
$16

Sweetbitter
Stacey Balkun
$16

Cosmobiological
Lilly Dreadful
$20

Dad Jokes from Late in the Patriarchy
Amorak Huey
$16

What Nothing
Anna Meister
$16

Where My Umbilical is Buried
Amanda Galvan-Huynh
$16

Kneel Said the Night
Margo Berdeshevsky
$20

the Colored page
Matthew E. Henry
$16

Year of the Unicorn Kidz
jason b. crawford
$16

Something Dark to Shine In
Inès Pujos
$16

Slaughter the One Bird
Kimberly Ann Priest
$16

The Valley
Esteban Rodriguez
$16

To Everything There Is
Donna Vorreyer
$16

Printed in the USA
CPSIA information can be obtained
at www.ICGtesting.com
JSHW052305300923
49025JS00006B/25